This book belongs to

_____

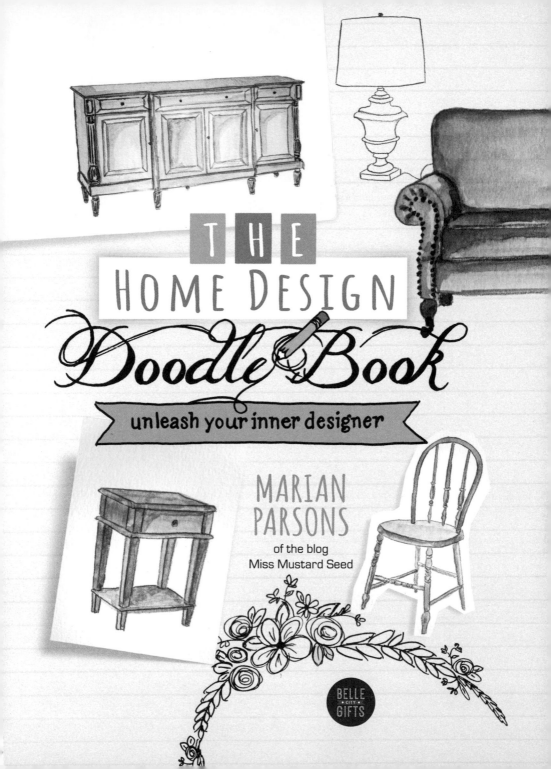

THE HOME DESIGN

Doodle Book

unleash your inner designer

MARIAN
PARSONS

of the blog
Miss Mustard Seed

BELLE
CITY
GIFTS

Belle City Gifts
Racine, Wisconsin, USA

Belle City Gifts is an imprint of BroadStreet Publishing Group, LLC.
Broadstreetpublishing.com

The Home Design Doodle Book

© 2017 by Marian Parsons

ISBN 978-1-4245-5413-3

All Scripture quotations are taken from the Holy Bible, New International Version®, NIV®. Copyright © 1973, 1978, 1984, 2011 by Biblica, Inc.™ Used by permission of Zondervan. All rights reserved worldwide. www.zondervan.com. The "NIV" and "New International Version" are trademarks registered in the United States Patent and Trademark Office by Biblica, Inc.™

Cover design by Chris Garborg | garborgdesign.com
Compiled by Kendall Moon.
Edited by Michelle Winger.

Printed in China.

17   18   19   20   21   22   23   7   6   5   4   3   2   1

TABLE OF CONTENTS

move mountains

in your

HOME

How to use This book

This book is not just a place to journal, dream, doodle, and plan. It's not just a notebook to store ideas, lists, and goals. This book is a <u>conversation</u>.

As you're writing down thoughts and hopes for your home, I will share my favorite tips, proven steps to decorating success, and encouragement. My voice is here to inspire you, give you confidence, and bring out your inner designer.

Think of me as your friend with a knack for decorating, and I will be right here with you as you coordinate fabric with paint colors and figure out arrangements. I have learned a lot in my 15-plus years of do-it-yourself-budget decorating, and I will share that experience with you.

There are no rules for using this journal, but I will offer up four suggestions:

1. This is a <u>doodle book</u>. You do not have to be an artist to put your ideas on paper, so let go...draw, doodle, color, and create! Every time you see this symbol , the page is waiting for your creative doodles.

2. There are <u>no mistakes</u>. You may draw things you don't like or make notes you don't follow, but they will all build into the designer you are becoming and the home you are creating. Resist the urge to rip out pages.

3. <u>You</u> <u>are</u> <u>creative</u>. Don't tell me you're not the "creative type." You were created in God's image, so you are creative by default. Use this journal to explore and discover new creative talents.

4. This is <u>your</u> book. I have shared a lot of ideas, prompts, sketches, and encouragement to get your creative wheels turning, but you are welcome to ignore those prompts, follow your own path, and add your personal touch to my doodles.

Please visit me online at http://missmustardseed.com/home-design-doodle-book/ where you can find even more helpful tips and creative inspiration.

Go forth and doodle!

Marian

What does your dream home look like?

dreams

your house right now

On the highly technical "thumbs up" scale,
show how you currently feel about your home...

Use five words that describe your
home right now...

Use five words to describe
what you want your home to be...

HOME GOALS

"Truly I tell you, if you have faith as small as a mustard seed, you can say to this mountain, 'Move from here to there,' and it will move. Nothing will be impossible for you."

MATTHEW 17:20

Creating your home isn't
an instant action.
It's a process.

I praise you because I am fearfully and wonderfully made;
your works are wonderful, I know that full well.

PSALM 139:14

Do nothing out of selfish ambition or vain conceit. Rather, in humility value others above yourselves, not looking to your own interests but each of you to the interests of the others.

PHILIPPIANS 2:3-4

Five steps to discovering your *style*...

One observe & collect

- Look through magazines, and search the internet. Save or print all of the images you love.

- Visit home décor stores and antique shops and take pictures or make notes of the things that speak to you.

- Resist the urge to buy! This is just a time to curate ideas.

By the grace of God I am what I am, and his grace to me was not without effect.

No, I worked harder than all of them—yet not I, but the grace of God that was with me.

1 CORINTHIANS 15:10

Two Filter what you love vs. what you love *for your home.*

"The grass withers and the flowers fall,
but the word of our God endures forever."

ISAIAH 40:8

Three recognize patterns...

Sketch or write out the things you are drawn to in each category.

color

furniture

what do your curated pictures & ideas have in common?

texture

decorating style

mood

Every good and perfect gift is from above, coming down from the Father of the heavenly lights, who does not change like shifting shadows.

JAMES 1:17

Four unearth your style

This is the fun part! It's time to find your style in your stuff.

Take time to go through your house and observe the contents with fresh eyes.

What I already have that works
with my newfound style

What I have that
doesn't fit

We remember before our God and Father your work produced by faith, your labor prompted by love, and your endurance inspired by hope in our Lord Jesus Christ.

1 THESSALONIANS 1:3

Five transition into your style

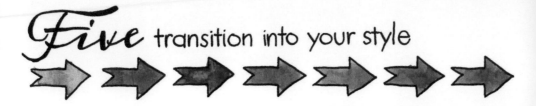

You have discovered your style. You have found what you already have that works in that style. Now it's time to transition your home, so that style is fully reflected in your home.

This is a process that may take weeks, months, or years. Just be patient, write out a plan, stay focused, and take it one step at a time.

She is clothed with strength and dignity;

she can laugh at the days to come.

PROVERBS 31:25

By wisdom a house is built, and through understanding it is established; through knowledge its rooms are filled with rare and *beautiful* treasures.

Proverbs 24:3-4

Be joyful in hope, patient in affliction, faithful in prayer.

ROMANS 12:12

Those who hope in the LORD will renew their strength. They will soar on wings like eagles; they will run and not grow weary, they will walk and not be faint.

ISAIAH 40:31

ROOM RESET

There are times when you need to start fresh with a room. Things just aren't feeling right and you need to hit the reset button. These five steps, my friend, are the way to hit that reset button. You will be amazed at how different a space can look in a day or two!

ONE everything out

Remove all accessories, wall art, textiles, small pieces of furniture, curtains, and rugs. This will allow you to see the bones of the room, so you can make a fresh decision about what should be in that room. This is a great time to sort though everything and declutter!

What do you notice about your room?

We are God's handiwork, created in Christ Jesus to do good works, which God prepared in advance for us to do.

EPHESIANS 2:10

TWO set the stage

Now that the room is empty, it's the perfect time to work on the large surfaces of the room—paint, bring in a new rug, clean the carpets, install moldings or built-ins, etc. This work is the foundation that sets the stage for the rest of the room.

Jot down arrangements you have tried, what worked and what didn't. This might help you down the road as you continue to perfect the space.

Wait for the LORD; be strong and take heart and wait for the LORD.

PSALM 27:14

THREE time to play

This is the time to rearrange your large furniture pieces! Play around with the arrangement and try all of your ideas, even if they seem a little nutty. This is playtime, and you may discover an entirely new way to use your room.

Change will feel "off" at first, but live with it for a few hours or even days before deciding if you love it or not.

What do you want as the foundation of your space? Neutrals? Lots of texture? A bold statement? Write down the direction you're heading, so you make sure your choices align with that end goal.

I pray that out of his glorious riches he may strengthen you with power through his Spirit in your inner being, so that Christ may dwell in your hearts through faith.

EPHESIANS 3:16-17

FOUR style

The walls are freshly painted,
the furniture is how you like it...
Now, it's time to bring in the accessories!

Play with pillows, throws, lamps, wall art, and knick-knacks. This is a great step to go through with a friend who can see your stuff with fresh eyes. Again, try everything that pops into your head! You can always modify it if you change your mind.

Did you find a new love for any of your accessories?

Did any changes surprise you?

"In the same way, let your light shine before others, that they may see your good deeds and glorify your Father in heaven."

MATTHEW 5:16

FIVE make lists

I have found that I often discover things I want to do or buy once a room reset is complete. I imagine you will, too! Make a list of those things, so as you're shopping or setting a home improvement budget, that list is handy and will keep you focused.

It's okay if this looks more like a "wish list." You might be surprised what you're able to source or accomplish as time passes.

Let the morning bring me word of your unfailing love, for I have put my trust in you. Show me the way I should go, for to you I entrust my life.

PSALM 143:8

Proverbs 31:13

She selects wool and flax and works with *eager hands.*

Whatever is true, whatever is noble, whatever is right, whatever is pure, whatever is lovely, whatever is admirable—if anything is excellent or praiseworthy—think about such things.

mood board

Wall color
"Glass Slipper"

- Antique blue and white quilts
- Ironstone pitchers in hutch
- Boxwood topiary behind sofa
- Woven tray for coffee table

Cow painting above buffet

Sofa fabric

Curtains— cream linen
"pinch pleat"

Braided jute rug

Pillow fabrics

Antique woven baske

Game and toy
storage (paint
in "Linen" milk
paint)

Slipcovers

layout

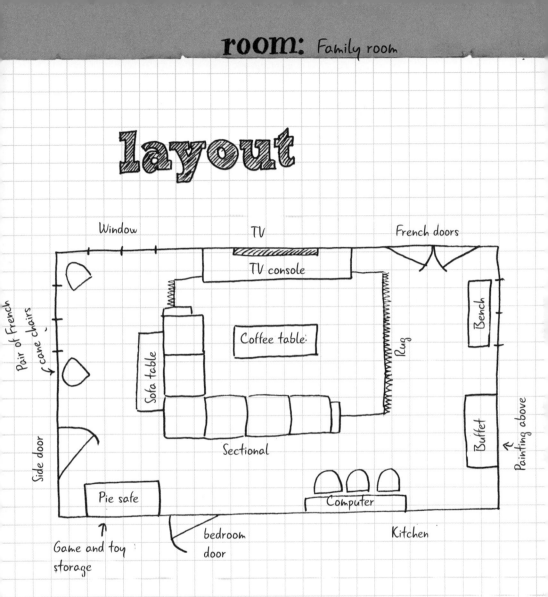

Window

TV

French doors

TV console

Pair of French cane chairs

Coffee table

Sofa table

Rug

Bench

Side door

Sectional

Buffet

Painting above

Pie safe

Computer

Game and toy storage

bedroom door

Kitchen

Casual, farmhouse feel, blue and white, antiques, texture, comfortable

41

mood board

layout

mood board

layout

mood board

layout

mood board

room: _____

layout

mood board

layout

mood board

layout

mood board

room: _____

layout

mood board

layout

mood board

layout

mood board

layout

mood board

layout

mood board

layout

There is no right or wrong when it comes to decorating.

There is only what you *love*.

To him who is able to do immeasurably more than all we ask or imagine, according to his power that is at work within us, to him be glory in the church and in Christ Jesus throughout all generations, for ever and ever! Amen.

EPHESIANS 3:20-21

Whatever you do, whether in
word or deed, do it all in the name
of the Lord Jesus, giving thanks to
God the Father through him.

COLOSSIANS 3:17

Let's go shopping...

shopping wish list

favorite
spots
to shop

antique shops

THRIFT
STORES

new places
to try

BUY IT...

- If it makes you smile
- If it's within your budget
- If it meets a functional need

List the qualities and characteristics
that are important to you in the items
you bring into your home.

DON'T BUY IT...

- If you don't love it and/or need it
- If it's beyond your ability (or time) to repair
- Just because it's a bargain

List your "don'ts" to help keep you focused and
reduce the chance of buyer's remorse.

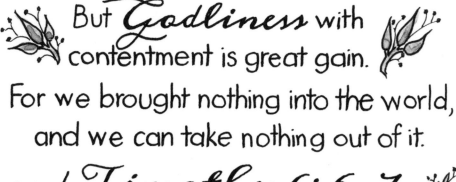

But *Godliness* with contentment is great gain. For we brought nothing into the world, and we can take nothing out of it.

1 Timothy 6: 6–7

You have many workers: stonecutters, masons and carpenters, as well as those skilled in every kind of work in gold and silver, bronze and iron—craftsmen beyond number. Now begin the work, and the LORD be with you.

1 CHRONICLES 22:15-16

We do not lose heart. Though outwardly
we are wasting away, yet inwardly
we are being renewed day by day.

2 CORINTHIANS 4:16

Home Decorating Tips

Selecting colors & coordinating fabrics

1. Select your inspiration piece. This can be anything! A rug, fabric, a painting, etc. Use this piece as your compass for the rest of the room.

2. Select the primary pattern for the room. This could be upholstered furniture, fabric, wall paper, a rug, etc.

3. Select fabric that coordinates with #1 and #2. A good rule of thumb is to have one all-over large pattern (like a floral), a geometric (like a check or stripe), and a solid. Feel free to be a rule-breaker though!

4. Paint colors are up next! Pick your colors for the walls, furniture, etc. This step comes later because you can find paint in thousands of colors and even have them custom mixed.

5. Bring in the accessories. Make sure you love each one and they support the other choices you have made.

Window dressings

If it's a casual space

Styles
Valances
Cornices

Fabrics
Cotton
Check
Plaids
Twill

If it's a formal space

Styles
Full-length drapes
Pinch pleats
Swags and jabots

Fabrics
Linen
Satin
Silk
Velvet
Toile
damask

"I have told you these things, so that in me you may have peace. In this world you will have trouble. But take heart! I have overcome the world."

JOHN 16:33

furniture

- Mix painted pieces with natural wood for an eclectic look.

- Form and function are both important. Each piece should be comfortable, practical, and look nice!

- If a piece is practical, but not pretty, how can you change that? Paint, slipcover, remove the doors, change the hardware?

- Make sure each piece is properly scaled for the room. Big room=large scale. Small room=small scale.

"The LORD bless you and keep you;
the LORD make his face shine on you and
be gracious to you; the LORD turn his face
toward you and give you peace."

NUMBERS 6:24-26

Furniture painting tips

1. Use a quality brush.

2. Use good paint.

3. If you're new to painting, start with a piece that's free or cheap.

4. Most pieces look worse before they look better!

5. Lightly sand the piece prior to painting to help paint adhere.

6. Make sure the piece is sturdy and worth painting.

7. It's just paint! You can fix just about anything with sandpaper.

For every house is built by someone,
but God is the builder of everything.

HEBREWS 3:4

Do not forget to show hospitality to strangers, for by so doing some people have shown hospitality to angels without knowing it.

Hebrews 13:2

Do everything in love.

1 CORINTHIANS 16:14

Flooring Checklist:

- Is it durable and practical for my family?
- Is it an appropriate choice for the room?
  (Think carpet in a kitchen or tile in a bedroom...)
- How is the floor cleaned and maintained? Will that work for me?
- Do I love it? (A floor is a big investment, and it takes up a
  lot of visual space.)

Under foot

He has filled him with the Spirit of God, with wisdom, with understanding, with knowledge and with all kinds of skills.

EXODUS 35:31

The 5th wall

Ceilings are often neglected, but they are considered the "5th wall." Paint the ceiling a surprising color, select a beautiful light fixture, or add an interesting architectural element like ceiling tiles or wood planks. What are some of your ideas for the ceilings in your home?

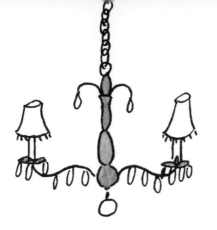

I will sing the
LORD's praise,
for he has been
good to me.
PSALM 13:6

lighting

General- Lights that flood the room to make it brighter. These are chandeliers, overhead lights, etc.

Task- Lights that are focused on a work surface like lamps, desk lights, under cabinet lights, etc.

Ambient- These lights provide mood. String lights, candelabras, and general lights on dimmer are all perfect for ambient lighting.

Do you have your lighting bases covered in each room?

"Everyone who hears these words of mine and puts them into practice is like a wise man who built his house on the rock."

MATTHEW 7:24

decorating & giving gifts

As you're decorating your home, pay attention to "gifts" you can give to your family (or even to yourself)! These are thoughtful, personal touches that make an individual feel like they are HOME.

What are some gifts you can give in your decorating?

A comfy chair?

A reading nook?

A displayed award?

The LORD has done it this very day; let us rejoice today and be glad.

Make every day special

Why save your fine china, silver, and linen napkins for "special occasions?" Get joy from them every day by putting them to use. It's a shame for our prettiest pieces to live in a buffet or hutch.

Now faith is confidence in what we hope for and assurance about what we do not see.

HEBREWS 11:1

You were created in the
Creator's image.

You are, by default, creative.

"When you enter a house, first say, 'Peace to this house.'"

LUKE 10:5

Collections

To give your collections greater visual impact,
group like things together!

"Be strong and courageous. Do not be afraid; do not be discouraged, for the LORD your God will be with you wherever you go."

JOSHUA 1:9

Hospitality

You may not know it, but your home is one of the best tools you have to minister to and encourage others!

What are ways you can use your home to bless friends, family, and strangers?

Share with the Lord's
people who are in need.
Practice hospitality.

ROMANS 12:13

Styling - the rule of 3

For some reason, things look better
when grouped together in threes
(or odd numbers). If you feel like
your styling never looks quite
right, try an arrangement with
three items of varying heights.

Give thanks in all circumstances; for this is God's will for you in Christ Jesus.

1 THESSALONIANS 5:18

the power of editing

Sometimes spaces are improved by what
we take away, not by what we add.

In their hearts humans plan their course, but the LORD establishes their steps.

Quick home refreshes...

- Add new pillows to a sofa, chair, or bed.

- Paint a piece of furniture.

- Add natural, seasonal touches like pinecones, sea shells, flowers, etc.

- Set your dining room table—cloth napkins and all!

- Style a bookshelf with pretty things as well as the books.

- Create a gallery wall with family pictures, favorite art, and mementos.

- Add a plant in a unique pot.

- Remove upper cabinet doors in your kitchen, and style your plates, bowls, mugs, and glasses.

You are altogether
beautiful, my darling;
there is no flaw in you.
SONG OF SONGS 4:7

Be thankful

When working on your home, it's easy to focus on what you don't have or what still needs to be done. Make sure you take intentional time to be thankful.

He has made everything beautiful in its time. He has also set eternity in the human heart; yet no one can fathom what God has done from beginning to end.

ECCLESIASTES 3:11

"For I know the plans I have for you," declares the LORD, "plans to prosper you and not to harm you, plans to give you hope and a future."

JEREMIAH 29:11

The entire law is fulfilled in keeping this one command: "Love your neighbor as yourself."

GALATIANS 5:14

Resources

decorating budget

Room:

Budget:

Actual $ spent:

Room:

Budget:

Actual $ spent:

Room:

Budget:

Actual $ spent:

Room:

Budget:

Actual $ spent:

Room:

Budget:

Actual $ spent:

Room:

Budget:

Actual $ spent:

Room:

Budget:

Actual $ spent:

Room:

Budget:

Actual $ spent:

Room:

Budget:

Actual $ spent:

Room:

Budget:

Actual $ spent:

Room:

Budget:

Actual $ spent:

Room:

Budget:

Actual $ spent:

Contractors

Name:

Contact Info:

Project and cost:

Notes:

Name:

Contact Info:

Project and cost:

Notes:

Name:

Contact Info:

Project and cost:

Notes:

Name:

Contact Info:

Project and cost:

Notes:

Name:

Contact Info:

Project and cost:

Notes:

Name:

Contact Info:

Project and cost:

Notes:

Name:

Contact Info:

Project and cost:

Notes:

Name:

Contact Info:

Project and cost:

Notes:

Name:

Contact Info:

Project and cost:

Notes:

Name:

Contact Info:

Project and cost:

Notes:

Name:

Contact Info:

Project and cost:

Notes:

Paint colors

Brand:

Color:

Finish:

Room/Furniture piece:

Brand:

Color:

Finish:

Room/Furniture piece:

Brand:

Color:

Finish:

Room/Furniture piece:

Brand:

Color:

Finish:

Room/Furniture piece:

Brand:

Color:

Finish:

Room/Furniture piece:

Brand:

Color:

Finish:

Room/Furniture piece:

Brand:

Color:

Finish:

Room/Furniture piece:

Brand:

Color:

Finish:

Room/Furniture piece:

Brand:

Color:

Finish:

Room/Furniture piece:

Brand:

Color:

Finish:

Room/Furniture piece:

Brand:

Color:

Finish:

Room/Furniture piece:

Fabrics

Maker:

Color:

Design:

Maker:

Color:

Design:

Maker:

Color:

Design:

Maker:

Color:

Design:

Maker:

Color:

Design:

Maker:

Color:

Design:

Maker:

Color:

Design:

Maker:

Color:

Design:

Maker:

Color:

Design:

Maker:

Color:

Design:

Maker:

Color:

Design:

Maker:

Color:

Design:

Maker:

Color:

Design:

Furniture & accessories

Piece:

Cost:

Brand/Store:

Finish:

Piece:

Cost:

Brand/Store:

Finish:

Piece:

Cost:

Brand/Store:

Finish:

Piece:

Cost:

Brand/Store:

Finish:

Piece:

Cost:

Brand/Store:

Finish:

Piece:

Cost:

Brand/Store:

Finish:

Piece:

Cost:

Brand/Store:

Finish:

Piece:

Cost:

Brand/Store:

Finish:

Piece:

Cost:

Brand/Store:

Finish:

Piece:

Cost:

Brand/Store:

Finish:

Piece:

Cost:

Brand/Store:

Finish:

do what you can
with what you have
where you are

—Theodore Roosevelt

A person can do nothing better than to eat and drink and find satisfaction in their own toil. This too, I see, is from the hand of God.

ECCLESIASTES 2:24

If we hope for what we
do not yet have, we wait
for it patiently.

ROMANS 8:25

You know the grace of our Lord Jesus Christ, that though he was rich, yet for your sake he became poor, so that you through his poverty might become rich.

2 CORINTHIANS 8:9

Do not forget to do good and
to share with others,
for with such sacrifices God
is pleased.

HEBREWS 13:16

Is your current home any closer to your dream home?
What new home-centered dreams do you have?

your house right now

Now that you've spent some focused time on your home,
how have your feelings about your house changed?

Use five words to describe your home right now...

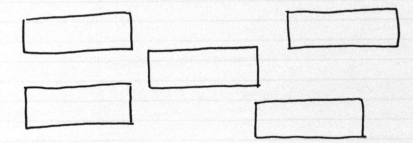

Compare these words to the ones you wrote in the beginning of this book.

If your home is right where you want it to be—AWESOME!

If not...keep working at it as time and budget allow. It's a process, and it's
okay if it takes a long time. Enjoy the journey!

home goals

Where do you want to go from here?

Mightier than the thunder of the great waters, mightier than the breakers of the sea—the LORD on high is mighty.

PSALM 93:4

Whatever you do,
work at it with all
your heart,

COLOSSIANS 3:23

as working for the
Lord...

He blesses the home
of the righteous.

PROVERBS 3:33

"Anyone who loves me will obey my teaching. My Father will love them, and we will come to them and make our home with them."

JOHN 14:23

author bio

Marian is a pastor's wife, mother of two little boys, paint and textile enthusiast, and lover of all things home. She started her business, Mustard Seed Interiors, in 2008, as a way to turn her love of decorating into extra money for groceries. What started as a local decorative painting and mural business has grown into a popular blog, Miss Mustard Seed blog (Miss Mustard Seed), an antiques and home décor business, and a paint line that is sold worldwide: Miss Mustard Seed's Milk Paint.

Marian's work has been featured in Country Living, Flea Market Style, Women's Day, Better Homes & Gardens, Fresh Style, Make It Over, Romantic Homes, Romantic Country, Farmhouse Style, Cottages & Bungalows, Fox News, NBC, CBS, and on the Nate Berkus Show. She currently lives near Gettysburg, PA, with her family and a parade of painted furniture.

Ready for more?

The final page of this book doesn't have to be the end of our conversations.

Decorating your home is a process, one that will continue long after your ideas, dreams, and plans are jotted down in this journal. You may also want fresh ideas and further instruction as you navigate new design trends and work toward turning your house into your dream home.

So let's hang out some more!

Miss Mustard Seed Blog
www.missmustardseed.com

Miss Mustard Seed on YouTube

Miss Mustard Seed on Facebook

@missmustardseed on Instagram

@missmustardseed on Twitter

Miss Mustard Seed on Pinterest

I hope to see you there!

Marian

aka: Miss Mustard Seed
Matthew 17:20